A Leopard Diary

My Journey into the Hidden World of a Mother and Her Cubs

This book is dedicated to Cathy Kays. Thank you for your support of this incredible project and for creating a safe haven for leopards and so many other species — S.E.

Owlkids Books acknowledges the financial support of the Canada Council for the Arts, the Ontario Arts Council, the Government of Canada through the Canada Book Fund (CBF) and the Government of Ontario through the Ontario Creates Book Initiative for our publishing activities.

Published in Canada by
Owlkids Books Inc.
1 Eglinton Avenue East
Toronto, ON M4P 3A1

Published in the United States by
Owlkids Books Inc.
1700 Fourth Street
Berkeley, CA 94710

Library of Congress Control Number: 2021951867

Library and Archives Canada Cataloguing in Publication

Title: A leopard diary : my journey into the hidden world of a mother and her cubs / by Suzi Eszterhas.
Names: Eszterhas, Suzi, author, photographer.
Identifiers: Canadiana 20210390964 | ISBN 9781771474917 (hardcover)
Subjects: LCSH: Leopard—Botswana—Pictorial works—Juvenile literature. | LCSH: Leopard—Infancy—Botswana—Pictorial works—Juvenile literature. | LCSH: Parental behavior in animals—Pictorial works—Juvenile literature.
Classification: LCC QL737.C23 E78 2022 | DDC j599.75/540222—dc23

Edited by Stacey Roderick
Designed by Danielle Arbour

Photo Credits: Page 4: Jak Wonderly (top); Emily2k/Dreamstime.com (bottom); 8: Dana Allen/Wilderness Safaris (top); 9: Dana Allen/Wilderness Safaris; 38: Kambango Sinimbo (both); 39: Children in the Wilderness (both).

Manufactured in Shenzhen, Guangdong, China, in April 2022 by WKT Co. Ltd.   Job # 21CB3195

A   B   C   D   E   F

Publisher of Chirp, Chickadee and OWL
www.owlkidsbooks.com | Owlkids Books is a division of bayard canada

A Leopard Diary

My Journey into the Hidden World of a Mother and Her Cubs

Suzi Eszterhas

Owlkids Books

Hi! My name is Suzi Eszterhas, and I am a wildlife photographer. I think it's the best job in the world!

My specialty is taking pictures of baby animals in the wild. I've traveled to some of the most remote places on Earth to photograph many different species, including lions, polar bears, gorillas, pangolins, penguins, and more. I often spend weeks or even months following the same animal family. That way I can photograph the babies as they grow up.

Leopards have always been one of my favorite animals. But they are very shy and skilled at hiding from humans, so this has made it hard to find a mother with young cubs to photograph. That's why I felt so lucky when I found out about the Camp Female, a very relaxed leopard that lives in the Jao Reserve in Botswana's Okavango Delta. The animals in this protected area are safe from hunters and have grown used to seeing people and safari vehicles. The Camp Female sounded like the perfect subject for my leopard photos. The only problem? She was not pregnant. Not yet anyway.

So I waited patiently for many months. When I finally received a message that she was noticeably pregnant, I was beyond excited! And I was even more excited weeks later when I was told the Camp Female had given birth! I quickly packed my bags and boarded a plane to Botswana.

My dream was coming true, and I wanted to remember this adventure forever. So I decided to keep this diary of my experiences.

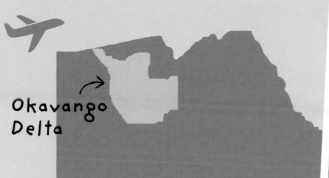

Okavango
Delta

BOTSWANA

Tubu Tree Camp is in the Okavango Delta in Botswana, a country in Southern Africa. The Okavango Delta is one of the world's largest wetlands. During the flood season, heavy rains from the mountains in neighboring Angola run down into the Delta, turning the camp into an island surrounded by water in July and August. The area teems with wild animals, including lions, wild dogs, elephants, giraffes, different kinds of antelopes, such as lechwes and kudus, and—of course—leopards!

April 19

I am so tired, but what an amazing day. It took nearly 40 hours of traveling, but here I am at the beautiful Okavango Delta!

When I got off the plane, my guide and tracker was there to greet me with the biggest smile—it turns out Kambango (he told me to call him Kam for short) was just as excited as I was! We went straight to the leopards' den while we still had a few hours of daylight. I had plenty of time to unpack and eat later.

Kam told me that the Camp Female had recently moved her two cubs. Leopard moms often do this to keep their young safe from predators, and I knew this was going to make things challenging for us.

A small hole in a fallen tree is a safe place for the cubs to stay when their mother is away. This way they are safe from large predators, such as baboons or lions. While Mom is gone, the cubs always stay close to the den so they can run inside if danger comes their way.

Her new den was covered with bushes and plants—she had hidden her cubs well. I needed to be patient if I wanted to catch my first glimpse of her and the cubs. After a couple hours, we heard a soft sound. It was the call a mother leopard makes for her cubs to let them know she is close by. She had been out hunting, and I could see that she had a full belly. Suddenly an adorable cub popped out of a nearby hole. And then another! They were so excited to see their mama!

But then she led them away, hiding them in the brush and out of our view. We decided to wait some more. It turned out to be worth it.

Finally we heard movement in the bushes. It was Mom with her two cubs following behind! She flopped to the ground, right where we could see her clearly. She checked us out for a moment and then rested her head on the grass. Bringing her cubs out in front of us meant she was relaxed, and it felt like she was giving us permission to see her cubs.

Only five weeks old, these beautiful, blue-eyed cubs are playful. They bounced, rolled, jumped, pounced, wrestled, and gently pawed at their mother. All right in front of us! I feel so lucky!

When Kam and I finally arrived at Tubu Tree Camp, it was just before dark. This will be my home while I'm here. It's a tent, but it feels like a palace! It is spacious and has beautiful furniture. Even better, when I walk out onto my veranda, I can see zebras and impalas grazing on the floodplains.

Both Kam (right) and his cousin Steve (left) work as guides and trackers. They are experts on the African bush, and they share their knowledge with guests on safari. Sometimes the animals they are tracking are hard to find, which means a lot of time can be spent searching for paw prints. It takes a trained eye to do this.

Kam and I had our dinner under the stars. He knows everything about this place. He told me that he was born and raised in the Delta. As a boy, he looked after his father's cattle and spent nights in the wilderness all on his own. He loves all wild animals, but he has a special connection to the Camp Female because he's followed her since she was two months old—just a little older than her cubs are now.

I can't wait for tomorrow. Somehow I have wound up at the most beautiful place in the world, with the best guide, photographing the most beautiful leopard mom. I feel like the luckiest person alive!

All the tents in the camp are connected by a raised boardwalk so people can walk around without having to worry about coming face-to-face with potentially dangerous animals, such as the elephants or lions that sometimes wander through camp.

April 20

This morning we were up early and headed straight to the leopards' den in the pitch-black darkness.

There were no signs of the leopards at first. But the bush was alive with birds singing the most beautiful songs while the sun came up. Kam knows each kind of bird. His favorite song is from the scrub robin. After hearing it sing, I can understand why.

After a couple hours, we heard rustling sounds at the den. Kam told me to get ready, and sure enough, Mom (as we call her now) slowly crept out into the open where we could see her. She was cautious and checked for danger before she called for her cubs to follow. Then just like yesterday, she stretched out on the thick green grass.

Leopard cubs are born with blue eyes that start to fade into a golden green when they are about eight weeks old.

The cubs were hungry! They began to suckle, but it wasn't long before they were fighting. Even though Mom had plenty of milk, they growled and swatted at each other before eventually settling down.

Afterward, the cubs climbed all over Mom while she tried to clean them. They seemed a bit more curious about us today and stared at me for a short time. I wondered how well they could actually see me. These cubs are so young that their eyesight is still developing.

Mom's tongue is rough like sandpaper. She uses it to detangle the cubs' fur and remove any parasites. This grooming also helps wash away strong odors that might attract the attention of predators.

Then it was playtime, and Mom's tail was clearly a favorite toy. The fuzzy, bright white fur on the tip kept the cubs' attention as she flicked her tail around. They chased it, caught it in their paws and mouths, and tugged on it as hard as they could.

After about an hour, the family returned to their hiding spot in the bushes. We didn't see them again for the rest of the day. That's okay. I'm so grateful for the quality time we had with them this morning and that I got some adorable photos of them playing.

April 23

Today we arrived at the den at sunrise. Mom was on a log with the cubs but left after only a few minutes. Kam said that she probably went to feed on a recent kill. It can take her up to three days to finish a meal, depending on the size of the animal.

While she was away, the cubs explored and played. They were full of energy again! They also tried out their climbing skills but didn't get very high before tumbling down. They definitely need more practice!

After lunch we went searching for Mom. I am learning so much from Kam. It can be easy to see paw prints in the sand, but he can even find tracks in the grass. And since Kam has followed the Camp Female for almost her whole life, he knows her favorite hunting spots. We checked those but still had no luck!

Leopards regularly hunt vervet monkeys, both on the ground and in the trees. When a vervet monkey sees a leopard, it will call to warn other monkeys. They have different calls for different predators, so the alarm for a leopard sounds different from the one they make for eagles.

Then at one point, we tried listening for alarm calls from other animals. Squirrels were screaming in the distance, but Kam said never to trust squirrels—they call out when they are fighting or when they see a snake. He said that kudu and vervet monkeys are more reliable—when they call out, it is usually because they have seen a leopard.

We never did find Mom, but we did see herds of giraffes nibbling on acacia trees, and a baby elephant at a water hole. You never know what you are going to see when you go on a safari drive!

Just before sunset, we decided to try the den again and saw one of the cubs in the bushes. It was a quick sighting, but at least we know the cubs are still there. I wonder if they are male, female, or one of each ...

During dinner, we heard kudu barking in alarm. Kam said that meant Mom was near. There is a water hole in camp, and she was probably thirsty after eating so much meat. All that searching today, and here was Mom, right under our noses!

April 26

There was no sign of the leopard family at the den this morning. Kam and I wondered if they were still sleeping, deep in the bushes. We waited for hours, but it was as if they had vanished.

We decided to drive around and look for their tracks. That's when Kam found Mom's large paw prints followed by tiny paw prints. They were leading away from the den, so we figured the family had moved to a new one in the night. The area was full of bushes and other great spots for a mother leopard to hide her cubs.

After looking for more tracks for another six hours in the scorching heat, we finally found the family! Their new spot was in a clearing between some thick brush. The cubs were busy pouncing on Mom, who was just trying to rest. They jumped on her head, wrestled her neck and tail, and leaped on her belly. It was hilarious to watch! And she was incredibly patient, despite a growl here and there.

Pouncing on Mom's head is fun for the cubs. For Mom? Probably not so much. But she knows this is important practice for stalking and ambushing prey. And a mother leopard also knows that play is essential for cubs to build strong muscles and develop coordination.

April 28

When we found the cubs this morning, they were playing. I could see that they have gotten stronger, even though they are still less than two months old. Now they can climb higher in the small trees and don't fall as often as they used to. They are also getting more aggressive when they play. There was snarling and growling today. At times it was so loud and fierce that it was hard to believe the sounds were coming from such little cubs!

They are even starting to hunt. They stalked butterflies a few times this morning. Maybe a butterfly will be the cubs' first kill ...

The cubs have grown too big to hide in small holes in logs and trees. Mom's new den is an island of bushes. There is a clearing for playing and resting when Mom is around, and deep brush for the cubs to hide in while she is away.

April 30

What a scare this afternoon!

We had parked our vehicle and given the leopard family plenty of space, like we always do. The cubs were playing in the bushes near us while Mom slept. Well, at one point, a cub fell out of the bush and startled Mom awake.

The cubs then crawled under our car. This upset Mom, who thought her babies were in danger.

We couldn't move the car because of the cubs underneath, so we stayed very still. She came to my side of the vehicle, sat down, and growled LOUDLY. I was terrified! My whole body was shaking! Kam stayed amazingly calm, which helped me stay calm. He told me to slowly lower myself in the seat. Mom kept growling.

Finally the cubs came out from under the vehicle, and Kam was able to start the car and slowly back away. Mom relaxed again and played with the cubs.

Writing this from the safety of my tent, I can't stop thinking about how scared I was. But I also know that the Camp Female is a wild animal who only wants to protect her babies. I want her to trust us and know that we would never do anything to hurt her or the cubs.

When frightened, leopards hiss or growl in warning. Humans need to give leopards plenty of space because they can become dangerous if they feel threatened. With their incredibly strong jaw muscles and razor-sharp claws, leopards can easily kill people.

May 3

Today we found Mom with her latest kill—a large male impala. It is amazing how strong she is. She used her mouth to pick up the dead animal and move it! I took photos as she dragged it into a bush to hide it from hyenas, lions, and wild dogs. With her impala safely stashed away, Mom would be able to feed for days.

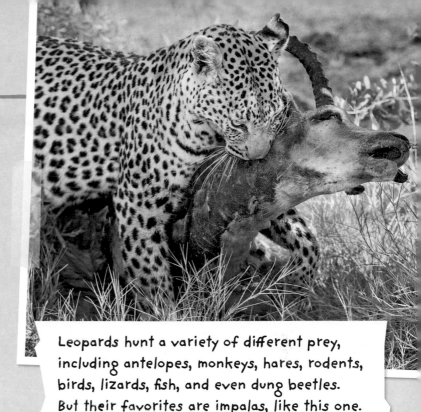

Leopards hunt a variety of different prey, including antelopes, monkeys, hares, rodents, birds, lizards, fish, and even dung beetles. But their favorites are impalas, like this one.

May 4

We had another scare this afternoon, but this time I was worried about the cubs' safety, not mine.

I think Mom was probably still with her impala meal, because the cubs were alone when some baboons feeding on the leaves of nearby bushes wandered into the den area! Knowing that baboons will kill even adult leopards, we were very afraid of the cubs being discovered. Luckily the cubs stayed quietly hidden in the thick bushes.

We held our breath as the baboons fed right near them. After what felt like ages, the baboons left, and our little cubs were safe!

I'd better get packed now because I leave for home tomorrow. I'll miss the leopard family, but I'll be back soon!

July 20

Kam picked me up when I landed this afternoon, and once again we went straight to find the leopards. Mom was off hunting, but we found the cubs.

In some ways it's like nothing had changed in the almost three months I've been gone. The cubs were up to their usual antics— chasing each other and climbing trees. But actually, so much *has* changed. I can't believe how much the cubs have grown. And Kam says that the cubs are now strong enough to travel much more with Mom. She still hides them in the bushes when she goes out hunting, but the family no longer uses a den, and sleeps in a different place every night.

It was good to see the cubs through my binoculars once again. They look healthy and strong! Kam thinks the cubs are both female, and I agree.

Tucked into bed in my tent now, I can hear the peaceful sounds of the African savanna. I am reminded how much I love this place—it is heaven!

July 21

We found the family all together this morning. The cubs were following Mom while she patrolled and marked her territory.

This is an important lesson for the cubs. If the family wanders out of this area, other leopards might attack them. And Kam says there is a female they call the Sand Gully Female who lives in the neighboring territory. She often fights with the Camp Female, and once even killed the cubs from the Camp Female's earlier litter!

Even though they are bigger now, the cubs are still small compared to an adult. I worry about them out in the open bush, no longer safely stashed away in a den. I hope these cubs are learning the boundaries of their territory!

This is the Sand Gully Female, the Camp Female's rival and a threat to the cubs. Leopards are solitary animals, except when they mate or have cubs. A leopard who crosses into another's territory is asking for a fight.

July 24

This morning we found Mom just after she had killed another impala. But before even taking a bite of her meal, she left to get the cubs.

While we were following her, we got a flat tire from acacia thorns. It's hard to believe a tree could have thorns so long and sharp that they can puncture a tire! Luckily Kam was able to change the tire in just three minutes, and we were back on her tail!

When Mom found her cubs, they wanted to play, but she was on a mission—there was a fresh meal waiting for them, and the family had to walk a long way to get to the kill.

One cub pounced belly first on top of the impala when they arrived. In my mind, I imagined the cub doing this as a fully grown, skilled hunter. For now, Mom was giving them a chance to learn and practice.

Mom had dragged the impala into some thick bushes so other predators would not find it while she was away. A fresh kill can attract lions, hyenas, and wild dogs—all of which are dangerous to a leopard and her cubs.

The cubs ate until they were full. Then they wandered down to a small pool of water for a drink. I took some pictures as they pawed playfully at the water. Seeing their reflections was still a new experience for them. I wondered if they recognized themselves ...

Next, the cubs began to groom. Mom will still lick them sometimes, but the cubs have learned how to clean themselves.

So after a big meal, a cool drink, and a quick bath, the cubs settled in for a long snuggle session with Mom. What could be better?

These cubs are discovering their world and learning the skills they need to survive in it. And once again I am grateful to be here to capture these moments with my camera!

Even though the cubs are older now, Mom still nuzzles and licks them. This touch is important for maintaining the mother-child bond—it keeps the cubs close by and therefore safe from danger.

July 25

I didn't sleep at all last night! Lions had killed an elephant right next to camp. That caused a loud war between the lions and the elephants all night long. The elephants trumpeted while the lions growled and called back. I felt sorry for the elephants, but I also know the lions need to eat and that they have cubs to feed. That's part of the circle of life. Sometimes it's sad, but I remind myself that nature has its own beautiful rhythm.

July 26

Leopards are arboreal, which means they spend a lot of time in trees. There are many good reasons for this. Being up high helps them avoid predators that hang out on the ground, such as lions and wild dogs. And the height makes it easier to spot vulnerable prey down below. Trees are also a great place to catch a cool breeze.

This morning the leopard family was resting when we found them. Mom was up high on a broken tree limb, and one cub was sleeping on a log below. But the other cub was lying on a pillow of elephant poop! It was both gross and adorable. And quite smart—it was probably a soft and cozy place to snooze.

While we watched, one of the cubs tried to join Mom on her perch. But she did not want to share. One growl was all it took for the cub to give up and find her own spot.

Tomorrow I have to return to the United States for some other work. It will be for a long time. Kam has promised to keep me up to date on how the cubs are doing, but I will still miss the family.

November 3

I'm glad to be back at Tubu, even for this short stay.

We searched all day for the leopard family but could not find them anywhere. Kam told me the family is moving more often and traveling farther than before. The cubs take longer strides now and have the energy to cover more of Mom's territory in a single day.

It was so hot, and we were out for nearly fourteen hours! We were both exhausted by the time we got back here to camp. But also happy to have been out in the bush again on such a beautiful day.

November 4

We searched all morning, again with no luck. Then in the afternoon we found the family!

The cubs are huge—almost the size of Mom! Their bodies are more muscular, too, which makes them look older. But it was good to see that the cubs are still as playful as ever.

Photographing them playing is so much fun! They run very fast now and pounce unexpectedly, so it is sometimes hard to keep them in focus.

November 5

The cubs have gotten so mischievous! After playing peekaboo around a termite mound, one of the cubs decided to play under our car. When I looked down, she stared right up at me and hissed.

We worried that Mom might think her cub was in trouble and get angry like the last time this happened. I wasn't quite as

scared, but just in case, we stayed perfectly still. Luckily Mom wasn't as scared either. She stayed resting peacefully and kept her cool. I'm glad she seems to trust us now.

Adult big cats like to stay cool in the shade of a vehicle on a hot day. And the cubs think it's a fun and different place to play! That's why Kam always makes sure he can see all members of the leopard family before he starts the car.

November 7

Mom killed another large female impala late this afternoon. It's a big meal that will keep the whole family fed for a few days. Kam and I talked about how hard it must be for her with two big cubs. She has to hunt more often and more skillfully, and kill enough food for herself *and* her cubs.

I'm going back home again tomorrow. I know that Mom will keep the cubs safe and healthy, and that they will keep growing and thriving while I'm away.

February 6

The cubs are almost one year old now. When I first saw them, they were tiny and helpless cubs. Now, one year and thousands of photos later, they are thriving!

Kam tells me a lot has changed in the months I've been gone. He says the cubs spend more time away from Mom and even some time away from each other. They often hang out in separate trees, but still close enough to know where the other is. This is all part of learning how to live without their mom and to be solitary cats.

February 7

I still can't quite believe what happened this morning.

Before dawn, while the world was still dark, I was walking along the boardwalk to get breakfast. Suddenly I saw something in front of me and turned my headlamp to see better. I was still so sleepy that I wondered if I was dreaming. Nope! It really was one of the leopard cubs. She was right there on the boardwalk! She looked at me, took a few steps away, stopped, and stared at me again.

I wasn't scared. I knew Kam had seen leopards on the boardwalk before and they hadn't been a threat to people, so I felt sure I'd be safe with the cub. We stared at each other a little while longer. She wasn't moving, but I had to get to breakfast! I tapped my boot lightly on the planks under my feet. As soon as the cub heard the sound, she jumped off the boardwalk.

What an incredible way to start the day! I told Kam that he didn't need to do any tracking today. I had already found the leopards!

February 9

The day began with a herd of kudu barking loudly in alarm nearby. We went straight to the sound. Mom had caught a kudu calf and given it to the cubs to chase for practice. It was very difficult to watch, but I know this is how cubs learn to catch and kill prey.

Cat mothers often bring prey to their young so they learn how to hunt by example. Pet cats are natural hunters, too. They chase toys that look like prey, and some also hunt for real prey such as birds, fish, bugs, mice, or other small rodents.

Later in the afternoon we watched as one of the cubs tried to hunt warthogs. The warthog family noticed the spotted predator right away and snorted in alarm. The cub's hunt was unsuccessful. I had to laugh when Kam said, "Those cubs are big, but they still have a lot of learning to do!"

Then later an amazing thing happened. While Mom and the cubs were dining on the kudu calf, a male leopard sneaked onto the scene. Kam and I held our breath—some male leopards kill cubs that aren't their own. But then Kam recognized the leopard—it was one of Mom's full-grown cubs from an earlier litter! What a surprise when Mom let him steal the kudu and run off with it. Kam says that some leopard mothers will still accept their older cubs.

Today was full of surprises! You never know what a day in nature will bring, and this is one of the things I love most about my job.

February 10

We tracked the family all day but didn't find them until this evening. It's harder now that they are covering more ground and on the move so much.

When we finally found them, they were hanging out together on a log during a beautiful sunset. Even though the cubs have become more independent, Mom still shows affection by grooming them.

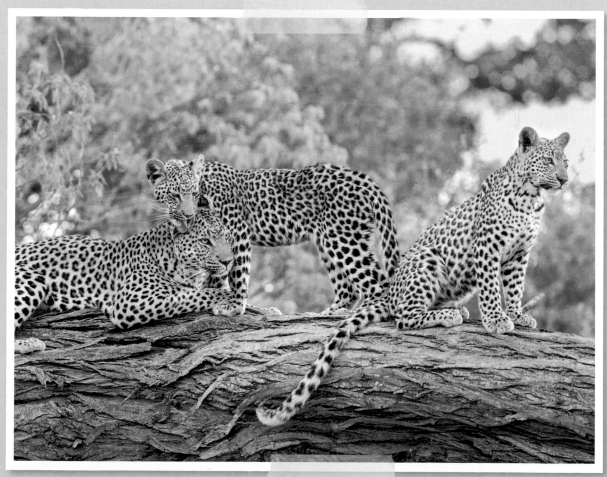

Sometimes Mom wants to play, too! While her cubs were trying to rest in the grass, she pounced! It all happened so fast, in just a fraction of a second. I was lucky to get this photo!

February 13

Wow, it was raining hard this morning! But we didn't want to miss the leopards so we went out anyway. Luckily the downpour didn't last long.

We found the cubs chasing each other in the long grass. After a rain shower, the cubs will often play for hours. Mom was having fun, too. In fact, she seemed even more playful than the cubs and was pouncing on them!

Later in the afternoon we were watching Mom climb a tall tree. One cub wanted to play, so she climbed up as well and jumped on top of Mom. I couldn't believe what happened next ... the branch they were on cracked in half and fell to the ground! Luckily the cub leaped to another branch, and Mom's cat reflexes allowed her to land on the ground safely on her feet. It was so unexpected and funny to see!

Like all cats, leopards have something called a "righting reflex," which is a natural ability to turn themselves during a fall so they land on their feet.

February 15

We searched all day for the family but couldn't find them. I was hoping to see them one more time before leaving tomorrow, but now I will have to wait until my next visit.

June 4

A lot has changed in the months I've been away. The cubs are now fifteen months old, and I'm shocked to see how big they are and how strong they look. They are nearly full-grown!

At sunrise we found them with a water mongoose that they had killed—without Mom's help! I'm happy to see that the cubs are hunting small animals for themselves, and that they are sharing meals with each other.

At this stage of life, the cubs are considered sub-adults (kind of like teenagers). They now spend most of their time away from Mom, and even each other, as they prepare for the solitary life of an adult leopard.

June 5

This afternoon we watched the cubs lounge together in the grass. They rested and stretched, and patted and nuzzled each other. But they aren't playing as much as they used to. They must realize how strong they are and don't want to accidentally hurt each other.

Kam said that for the last couple months, the cubs have often been away from Mom. She still calls them when she has food to share, but that is the only time they are all together. He explained that the cubs are almost ready for life on their own, and Mom is preparing for her next litter.

When I asked Kam if he thought we'd be able to photograph Mom with her next litter, he said, "That will be very challenging, but I can't wait to try!" So now we've hatched a plan: I will return to Tubu to photograph Mom's next cubs, this time while they are newborns! Kam is going to keep watch and let me know when she is pregnant again.

Mom will have another litter soon. In the wild, leopards can have cubs every two years.

February 22

The Camp Female has a new litter!

Kam was right—this is going to be our biggest challenge yet. Very few people on Earth have seen a newborn leopard cub in the wild, and it won't be easy.

But I am so happy to be back. Tubu feels like my second home now. I know everyone here so well, they feel like old friends. Especially Kam.

February 23

We spent all day at the den site. We watched Mom leave and return. Then we heard the soft sounds of a cub nursing! And since we didn't hear any of the growling that often happens between siblings, Kam is sure there is only one cub.

The cub was hidden inside a log on the ground, deep under a cover of thick bushes. We tried to see what it was doing, but our binoculars were of no use.

Mom stashed her newborn cub deep inside this bush. Lions, wild dogs, hyenas, jackals, and baboons prey on leopard cubs, so they need to be really well hidden.

February 24

We spent all day at the den again. Still no sign of the cub. But while we waited, some fish eagles flew by—their call has become one of my favorite sounds of the African bush. We also watched as a lilac-breasted roller hunted for insects in the grass and dung beetles rolled their dung balls.

February 26

This morning we found Mom in a tree, looking around for a new location. Kam had predicted that she would move the cub today, and he was right. Sometimes I think he is a wizard!

Mom went back into the den and came out with the cub in her mouth. As she carried it gently by the scruff of its neck, we could see that it was a boy! She walked what was about the length of a football field to a new bush and disappeared inside.

Leopard moms move their newborn cubs every few days. If they stay in the same spot too long, predators might smell or hear the cubs.

February 28

This morning we found lion tracks near the den site! I was worried because lions are a great threat to leopards, especially cubs. We looked all day but didn't find Mom or her cub. Kam thinks she has moved her den because of the lions.

February 29

We were out tracking when we got a radio call from the Tubu camp manager. He explained that a staff member had "found a leopard cub in the camp bathroom!" Kam and I laughed. We assumed this person had mistaken a genet for a leopard cub since both animals are small and spotted. But we were also curious, so we headed back to camp.

We went to investigate, and there behind the sink, curled up against the wall, was a tiny, furry ball of spots! I could hardly believe my eyes—it was the two-week-old leopard cub! I quickly snapped some photos. He was old enough to see me as a threat and told me so with a tiny hiss.

Kam and I did not want to stress out the cub and we had no idea where Mom was, so we left the bathroom. Mom may be relaxed and familiar with us out in the grassland, but this was her new den and she would be ferocious if she found us too close to her cub.

We moved a safe distance away and waited for Mom. Why would she hide her baby in such a strange place? Kam explained that this camp is part of her territory. And this side of camp has no guests, so it is very quiet and dark. Also, this leopard mom was smart enough to know that lions avoid walking on the camp's raised boardwalk, so they would never find her cub in the bathroom.

When Mom finally returned to the camp, she relaxed by the swimming pool, took a drink, and then sauntered up to find her cub. We heard her call quietly as she entered the bathroom. She reappeared with the cub in her mouth and carried him out of camp to stash him in a hollow log in a thicket.

Mom carried the cub in her mouth down the boardwalk and through the bush before finally dropping him into a safe hole in a log that was well hidden.

I'm relieved she found a more natural den, but it was amazing to witness a wild animal trust humans so much. It is something that I will always remember.

I'm leaving for home tomorrow. Even though I know it will be a long time before I come back, I'm lying here tonight with a full heart. I feel sure that Mom will raise this little cub to adulthood, just like the other two cubs. I'll be looking for him on my future visits. And hopefully when he grows up, he'll be a father of cubs—another generation of leopards at Tubu. Maybe I will be fortunate enough to be able to photograph them!

The cub peeked out of his new hiding spot after his adventure in the camp bathroom.

A Conversation with Kambango

Without Kam's help and expertise, it would have been very hard for me to find and take photos of the Camp Female and her cubs. The more time I spent with him, the more fascinating I found his work. Here are some of the questions I had for him:

What do you do in your job as a guide and tracker?

As a guide and tracker I help other people experience the African bush. When you are out in nature you must wake up all your senses and use your eyes, ear, and nose to find animals. And you need patience to allow the animals to reveal themselves.

How did you become a guide and tracker? How did you learn or study to do this job?

I read a lot of books about wildlife and went to a training program to become an official guide. But during this program I found I had an advantage because I grew up in the bush and already knew much of what they were teaching. So my studies were easy.

What is the best part of your job?

I love being in the Delta—the water and the wildlife make me feel so good. I especially like being on the water in our traditional boats called mokoros (a kind of canoe that you paddle while standing up). Nothing is better than floating peacefully through the grass, so close to animals such as elephants.

What is your favorite animal to track, and why?

The leopard is my favorite animal. You often have to work really hard to find them but when you do it is always rewarding. I never get tired of watching them. I can sit and watch a leopard for a whole day and be happy.

What is the scariest thing that has ever happened to you in the bush?

I was once chased by a hippo while I was driving a boat. He was in the water and came out of nowhere. He lunged at the boat, and I couldn't go very fast to escape from him because the channel was narrow. He kept coming after me, over and over again, and nearly got me. Hippos are one of the most dangerous animals in Africa, so it was very, very scary.

A Bit About Children in the Wilderness

In addition to his work as a guide, Kambango works with Children in the Wilderness (CITW). CITW is a non-profit organization that hosts rural children who live close to Wilderness Safaris reserves and teaches them the importance of conservation through programs such as Eco-Clubs, the YES Programme, and Eco-Mentor training. The children are exposed to local wildlife and nature, which helps build and strengthen their ability to cope with life's challenges. They are taught the life skills necessary to reach their greatest potential so that they are equipped to become the future custodians of these pristine wilderness areas.

Words to Know

acacia tree: a tree that grows in warm climates and is known for its large, sharp thorns

arboreal: a word used to describe animals that spend much of their time in trees

delta: an area of low wetland that forms where a river empties into a larger body of water

genet: a small carnivore that resembles a cat, but is more closely related to a mongoose

guide: a skilled expert who escorts tourists and visitors safely around parts of the savanna

reserve: an area of land where wild animals are protected from humans, particularly hunters and poachers

safari: a trip people take, usually in African countries, to see animals in their natural habitats

savanna: a grassland ecosystem that has warm temperatures year-round and a rainy season

solitary animal: an animal that lives mainly on its own, rather than with others of its species

suckle: the way a young mammal feeds on its mother's milk by sucking

territory: an area that an animal marks and protects as its own

tracker: a trained expert who finds and follows wild animals using knowledge of animal tracks, sounds, habits, and more